# Canadian Slang Sayings and Meanings: Eh!

## David LaChapelle

I thank my family for their interest and contributions in this book: My Dad for getting on board with this project, Betty for her input, my mother for her additions and my brother Steven for creating such a wonderful cover. To all my readers and fans out there: I thank you from the bottom of my heart for giving me a purpose in life. God bless.

# INTRODUCTION

You may wonder what kind of English that Canadians are speaking. Every culture has its slang sayings and we are no exception. Many people in Canada may not even know that they are using slang, and this collection of sayings is to bring awareness of a hidden language.

In this book there is quite a collection of slang sayings and their meanings and is organized by a number system for easy referencing. The meanings are described in a clear, concise and simple manner. Where more detail was required, I did the best I could to draw out the true meaning of the saying. I hope you enjoy this creation of mine inspired by Canadians and those who want to learn Canadian English or broaden their slang vocabulary. Enjoy.

*Slang Saying = SS*

*Meaning = M*


SS1: Pretty penny

M1: A lot of money


SS2: Gone to the dogs

M2: Deteriorated


SS3: Gone downhill

M3: Deteriorated


SS4: Fools gold

M4: Fake wealth


SS5: Book worm

M5: Book lover

SS6: She is hot out there

M6: It is hot outside


SS7: I got wheels

M7: I have an automobile


SS8: Last call

M8: Last time to get alcohol at a bar


SS9: Mother load

M9: Large load


SS10: Fancy free

M10: No responsibilities


SS11: It is not what it is cracked up to be

M11: Does not meet expectations

SS12: On the tip of my tongue

M12: I can almost remember what to say


SS13: Lip service

M13: Telling someone what they want to hear

   but do not mean it


SS14: At your fingertips

M14: Within proximity or range


SS15: Heat score

M15: Attracting trouble or bad attention


SS16: Pencil pusher

M16: Office worker

SS17: Keep on keeping on

M17: Continue in what you are doing


SS18: Give me the dough

M18: Give me the money


SS19: Give me some coin

M19: Give me some money


SS20: Don't be crabby

M20: Don't be irritable


SS21: Grand father clause

M21: New certification or license rules do not

apply to you because you were there

before the new regulations took place

SS22: Chick magnet

M22: A person who attracts the attention of

women

SS23: Hiding under the air

M23: Cooling off under the air conditioner

SS24: Last leg

M24: Last chance or effort

SS25: Rattled my cage

M25: Disturbed and unsettled

SS26: Ice breaker

M26: An opening statement or object that

creates rapport with a stranger

SS27: Breaking the ice

M27: Working on finding something in

common and being comfortable with a

stranger


SS28: They have guts

M28: They have courage


SS29: Hot dog

M29: How about that?


SS30: Half in the bag

M30: Not fully aware or awake


SS31: Under dog

M31: A person or team that is not expected to

win

SS32: Don't make a mountain out of a mole hill

M32: Don't make something out of nothing


SS33: Kickback

M33: A perk or reward on top of one's wages for doing their duty or job


SS34: You are on a roll

M34: Successfully tackling challenges one after another


SS35: You cannot pull the wool over my eyes

M35: To deceive


SS36: Don't weasel your way out

M36: Don't back out of a commitment

SS37: Have a beef

M37: Complaint


SS38: Watch your p's and q's

M38: Be careful


SS39: You sound like a broken record

M39: Repeating yourself


SS40: That is money

M40: Success


SS41: Hang tight

M41: Be patient


SS42: Hang in there

M42: Be patient

SS43: Make it or break it

M43: Win or lose everything


SS44: Fix your wagon

M44: Correct someone


SS45: Will you sleep with me?

M45: Do you want to have sex


SS46: Will you go to bed with me?

M46: Do you want to have sex


SS47: Don't be a chicken

M47: Don't be a coward

SS48: Pickup line

M48: An opening statement to impress

someone you want to have relations

with


SS49: No skin of my ass

M49: Not a burden for me


SS50: Beauty is in the eye of the beholder

M50: A person's attraction to another is

diverse and differs from person to

person


SS51: The midnight hour

M51: The end point to do something

SS52: You have a voice like an angel

M52: A very good voice


SS53: What is up?

M53: What is new


SS54: White collar worker

M54: Non physical worker


SS55: Blue collar worker

M55: Physical labor worker


SS56: What is brewing?

M56: What is happening


SS57: A mile a minute

M57: Very fast

SS58: They are a loaded gun

M58: Their temper could explode at any

   moment


SS59: I can run circles around you

M59: I am better than you


SS60: They are shell shocked

M60: Devastated


SS61: Picture perfect

M61: Ideal result or situation


SS62: For the millionth time

M62: I have told you enough times already

SS63: Aced it

M63: Easy success


SS64: Higher stakes

M64: More to win or more to lose


SS65: Scared to death

M65: Really scared


SS66: Sailing

M66: Searching for yard or garage sales


SS67: The final piece of the puzzle

M67: Conclusion


SS68: Consider it a loss

M68: A lesson in life

SS69: You have been sold down the river

M69:  You have been taken advantage

of


SS70: If the shoe fits let them wear it

M70: Let a person be what they are


SS71: It seems we are playing musical chairs

M71: People switching or changing seats


SS72: You're the apple of my eye

M72:  You mean a lot to me


SS73: Have a whale of a good time

M73: Have a great time

SS74: Do not beat around the bush

M74: Get to the point or conclusion

SS75: Been around the block

M75: Have experience

SS76: Not a happy camper

M76: Not a happy person

SS77: It seems we are playing mental chess

M77: Overworking your brain

SS78: Washed under the bridge

M78: Forgotten

SS79: I will sleep on it

M79: I will think about it

SS80: Out of the blue

M80: Unexpectantly


SS81: Turn it down

M81: Reject it


SS82: Joe blo

M82: Anybody


SS83: A rolling stone gathers no moss

M83: Don't stagnate and keep being active in

life


SS84: Right off the bat

M84: A good start with no hesitations

SS85: Do you dig it

M85: Do you like it


SS86: Strikes your eye

M86: Attracted to it


SS87: You bet

M87: For sure


SS88: Hit the bottle

M88: Turning to alcohol drinking


SS89: Turning over a new leaf

M89: A new beginning in life


SS90: Not picking this out of thin air

M90: True

SS91: Go hot rodding

M91: Go racing


SS92: Closing its doors

M92: End of a business


SS93: What the hell?

M93: Why?


SS94: Dirt cheap

M94: Real inexpensive


SS95: Rust bucket

M95: A vehicle that has a lot of rust


SS96: Upper crust person

M96: Upper class person

SS97: Sharp cookie

M97: A smart person


SS98: Flows out of your mouth

M98: Easy to speak


SS99: There is light at the end of the tunnel

M99: Hope


SS100: Think twice

M100: Be sure or do not do it


SS101: Did not bat an eyelash

M101: Did not hesitate


SS102: Hit the road

M102: Get driving

SS103: Hit the floor

M103: Astonished


SS104: Talk to the hand

M104: I am not listening


SS105: It is a walk in the park

M105: Easy


SS106: Touch base

M106: Talk to me and keep in touch


SS107: Smoke another one

M107: I do not believe you


SS108: Hands full

M108: Busy with responsibilities

SS109: Drink their faces off

M109: Consuming a lot of alcohol


SS110: Heat score

M110: Target for trouble or negative attention


SS111: I do not feel so hot

M111: I do not feel well or good


SS112: Open a can of worms

M112: Revealing secrets and releasing burdens


SS113: Veg out

M113: To vegetate, being inactive or not
doing anything

SS114: Do not leave me hanging

M114: Do not leave me alone or give no

answer

SS115: For the love of God

M115: I cannot believe that just happened

SS116: A down to earth person

M116: Friendly person

SS117: Under your belt

M117: An experience you have

SS118: That is money

M118: Good idea

SS119: Plan B

M119: Backup plan


SS120: Bender

M120: Drinking alcohol for a period of time


SS121: Got my work cut out for me

M121: Have a job to do


SS122: I'm coffeed out

M122: Had too much coffee


SS123: Happy medium

M123: Compromise


SS124: Chit chat

M124: Quick conversation

SS125: Small talk

M125: Conversation about nothing in

particular

SS126: Shoot the shit

M126: Small talk

SS127: Get your ducks in order

M127: Organize

SS128: Pinky finger

M128: Baby finger

SS129: Puppy love

M129: Young people in love

SS130: Liquid lunch

M130: Beer for lunch


SS131: That is all it boils down too

M131: Come to a conclusion


SS132: Runs in the family

M132: Evident throughout the family


SS133: Do not be a suck

M133: Do not be immature


SS134: Do not be a baby

M134: Be mature

SS135: Cross the line

M135: Did or said something that you should
not have


SS136: Do not rock the boat

M136: Do not disturb what is settled


SS137: Stand out like a sore thumb

M137: Real noticeable


SS138: Drawing a blank

M138: Cannot think of anything


SS139: Strong as an ox

M139: Very strong

SS140: When pigs fly

M140: Never


SS141: Blowing steam

M141: Releasing built up pressure in a person


SS142: Do not blow your horn

M142: Do not brag


SS143: Coughing my brains out

M143: Coughing a lot


SS144: Smoke your brains out

M144: Smoking a lot


SS145: Bored stiff

M145: Really bored

SS146: Lose your cool

M146: Lose you temper


SS147: Cannot put my finger on it

M147: Cannot figure it out


SS148: Beat me to the punch

M148: Got there first


SS149: Not out the woodwork yet

M149: Still more to do


SS150: Odds and ends

M150: A little bit of everything


SS151: Rings a bell

M151: I remember that

SS152: Throw the book at you

M152: The law is not in your favor


SS153: Short end of the stick

M153: Whatever is leftover


SS154: No strings attached

M154: No commitments or responsibilities


SS155: Your eyes will light up

M155: You will like it


SS156: Things will iron out

M156: Things will work out


SS157: Counting sheep

M157: Trying to go to sleep

SS158: Up the creek

M158: In trouble


SS159: Too much time on my hands

M159: Do not know what to do with yourself


SS160: Talk is cheap

M160: Speak what you can support


SS161: Put your money where your mouth is

M161: Prove it


SS162: Sticking to your guns

M162: Staying with your convictions


SS163: Swinging in different circles

M163: Hanging around different friends

SS164: Shitting bricks

M164: Really scared


SS165: Part of the program

M165: Expected


SS166: Empty nest

M166: Grown children moved out of parent's

home for the first time


SS167: Mover and groover

M167: Active in the social scene


SS168: Fudge the numbers

M168: Fraud

SS169: Curb your appetite

M169:  Control your hunger


SS170: Going overboard

M170: Doing too much


SS171: The jury is still out

M171: Undecided


SS172: Open the gates

M172: Welcome them


SS173: Not out of the woods yet

M173: Not safe yet


SS174: It is in my blood

M174: I live for it or love it

SS175: A rock and a hard place

M175: Difficult position to be in


SS176: Loose lips sinks ships

M176: Gossip hurts other people


SS177: Lost for words

M177: Do not know what to say


SS178: Sitting on top of the world

M178: Doing well, success


SS179: Clunker

M179: An old vehicle not in good condition


SS180: Horny as a toad

M180: Oversexed

SS181: Save money for a rainy day

M181: Save money for when you may need it


SS182: An old wreck

M182: An old vehicle not in good condition


SS183: Puff up your chest

M183: Be proud


SS184: In the ballpark

M184: You are close


SS185: Change your tune

M185: Change your opinion or attitude


SS186: Long time no see

M186: I have not seen you in awhile

SS187: Chip in together

M187: Contribute or donate together


SS188: Put on your thinking cap

M188: Come up with some ideas


SS189: Went through the floor

M189: Shocked


SS190: Did you break wind

M190: Did you fart


SS191: It is a win, win situation

M191: Can't go wrong either way


SS192: Put me through the ringer

M192: Put me through hardships

SS193: Put me to the test

M193: Try me


SS194: Can't win for losing

M194: Just cannot win


SS195: Swear like a trooper

M195: Foul mouth


SS196: Light on their feet

M196: Graceful


SS197: Spill your guts out

M197: Express your deep feelings


SS198: Hurts your pocketbook

M198: Cost you money

SS199: More salt in the wounds

M199: More emotional injury to a hurting person

SS200: Right to the tee

M200: Exact

SS201: Tit for tat

M201: Equal exchange

SS202: Add insult to injury

M202: Made things worse

SS203: Bite the bullet

M203: Take responsibility

SS204: Clean ship

M204: Move people around


SS205: Hands in the pocket

M205: Stealing from someone


SS206: In good spirits

M206: Feeling good


SS207: Dryer than a bone

M207: Very dry


SS208: Throw up the white flag

M208: Surrender


SS209: Up and down like a yo-yo

M209: Unstable and unpredictable

SS210: Get your tongue around it

M210: Express the idea


SS211: Right up your alley

M211: Something that you would like


SS212: Jumping the gun

M212: Getting ahead too soon


SS213: Laying down the law

M213: Establishing personal boundaries


SS214: Put your foot down

M214: Establishing personal boundaries


SS215: Do not let it burn a hole in your pocket

M215: Do not have to spend your money

SS216: Dough

M216: Money


SS217: Down the toilet

M217: Gone to waste


SS218: Down the drain

M218: Gone to waste


SS219: So close, I could almost taste it

M219: Very close


SS220: Get to the bottom of it

M220: Investigate


SS221: Always in the picture

M221: Involved

SS222: I make peanuts

M222: Earn very little wages or money

SS223: Basket case

M223: Mentally unstable

SS224: Hung up on them

M224: I like them

SS225: Dialed in

M225: Focused

SS226: Hung over

M226: Feeling ill from alcohol consumption

SS227: Did you pass gas

M227: Did you fart

SS228: What the heck?

M228: Why?


SS229: Just collecting dust

M229: Not using it


SS230: Watch your back

M230: Be careful of others


SS231: Keep to myself

M231: Stay away from others


SS232: Drop them like a hot cake

M232: End a relationship quickly


SS233: On the flip side

M233: The positive viewpoint

SS234: Off to the races

M234: Going out


SS235: Shout out

M235: Public announcement


SS236: That ship has sailed

M236: It is too late


SS237: Take a pill and chill

M237: Relax and be patient


SS238: They know how to push your buttons

M238: They know how to upset you


SS239: I am going to hold on to my teeth

M239: Staying confident

SS240: I will sit on it

M240: I will think about it


SS241: No two ways about it

M241: For sure


SS242: No if's, and's or but's

M242: For sure


SS243: The show is over

M243: Nothing to look at here


SS244: Let's get this show on the road

M244: Let's get going

SS245: You burnt your bridges

M245: Ended relationships you cannot go

back too

SS246: It is out of my hands

M246: Out of my control

SS247: They hung you out to dry

M247: Ignored you with no help

SS248: God speed

M248: In good time

SS249: Looking for an easy out

M249: Looking for an easy way to get out of

something

SS250: There is a spark between us

M250: There common attraction or

connection

SS251: Weird duck

M251: Weird person

SS252: They would not hurt a fly

M252: Harmless

SS253: They warmed up to me

M253: Friendly

SS254: Write them off

M254: Do bother with them anymore

SS255: Go big or go home

M255: Give it all or nothing


SS256: Bottom of the barrel

M256: At the very bottom


SS257: A nutbar

M257: A crazy person


SS258: Under the table

M258: Hidden or working for cash


SS259: It is a rocky road

M259: Experiencing difficulties


SS260: I am not just a pretty face

M260: I am smart too

SS261: Beside myself

M261: In disbelief


SS262: Fit as a fiddle

M262: Very fit


SS263: Go off the deep end

M263: Lose all control and hope


SS264: Bird's eye view

M264: Full perspective


SS265: Further in the hole

M265: Further in financial debt


SS266: I am feeling down

M266: Feeling not good

SS267: I am feeling up

M267: Feeling good


SS268: I feel like a rock star

M268: I feel popular


SS269: White lies

M269: Little seemingly insignificant lies


SS270: Lick my wounds

M270: Comfort and recover myself


SS271: Hanging on for dear life

M271: Just surviving


SS272: Market cornered

M272: Ahead of competition

SS273: Out to lunch

M273: Not mentally fit


SS274: The clock is ticking

M274: Not much time left


SS275: You got carded

M275: Had to show identification


SS276: Back to the drawing board

M276: Back to the beginning


SS277: Blew my mind

M277: Above expectations


SS278: Bummed out

M278: Depressed

SS279: Going through the motions

M279: Repeating mundane work or life


SS280: Be careful what you wish for

M280: Might come true


SS281: Been through the mill

M281: Experienced difficulties


SS282: Don't drag my name through the mud

M282: Don't give me a bad reputation


SS283: That is cheap

M283: Low quality


SS284: Like a fish out of water

M284: Out of comfort zone

SS285: That's hot air

M285: Not truthful


SS286: Put your best foot forward

M286: Make you best effort


SS287: One step forward and two steps back

M287: Not getting ahead


SS288: Their nuts

M288: Their crazy


SS289: Circling numbers

M289: Playing the lotto


SS290: You drag yourself around

M290: Extending yourself when tired

SS291: You light up my life

M291: You bring happiness to my world


SS292: Time and tide waits for no person

M292: Get going


SS293: Their an emotional wreck

M293: Disturbed and upset


SS294: Don't have a fiddler's chance

M294: No chance


SS295: She has a feather in her hat

M295: Upper class woman


SS296: Drive you around the bend

M296: Make you crazy

SS297: Ahead of the game

M297: Have advantage


SS298: Don't stand a ghost of a chance

M298: No chance


SS299: Going squirrely

M299: Going crazy


SS300: Rack your brains

M300: Thinking hard


SS301: Open your eyes.

M301: Being able to see reality and the truth

SS302: I would not give him the time of day.

M302: Would not show attention or talk to
  him.

SS303: Off the top of my head.

M303: Just instantly thought about it

SS304: Whole nine yards.

M304: All the way.

SS305: The lights are on but nobody's home.

M305: A person who is not 100 percent
  mentally fit.

SS306: It is so old it has hair on it.

M306. It Is really old.

SS307: Just wing it.

M307: Just improvise.


SS308: It is a nail biter of a game.

M308: It is a close game.


SS309: It is a two-way street.

M309: If you are going to take from

somebody, you have to give as

well, as it goes both ways.


SS310: It is an open-door policy.

M310: You can have free access to upper

management


SS311: Do not get your nose out of joint.

M311: Do not get upset or offended.

SS312: You might as well bury the hatchet.

M312: You might as well forgive and forget.


SS313: You have swept it under the rug.

M313: You have put aside and away

　　　　differences to be forgotten and out of

　　　　sight.


SS314: Let it slide.

M314: Forget about it.


SS315: Second hand car.

M315: Used car.


SS316: It is in black and white.

M316: It is clear and evident.

SS317: Cook the books.

M317: Making false financial reports to look

better than what they are.


SS318: That is cheesy.

M318: That is out of style.


SS319: That is corny.

M319: That is out of style.


SS320: That is a pipe dream.

M320: That is an unrealistic dream.


SS321: Take them with a grain of salt.

M321: Do not take them seriously and

take the good with the bad.

SS322: You catch more bees with honey

than with vinegar.

M322: You attract more good people by

being nice than not being nice.

SS323: That is blue murder.

M323: That is a real injustice

SS324: Slipping through the cracks.

M324: A person being failed by the

government system.

SS325: Blood is thicker than water.

M325: Family bonds are stronger than friends.

SS326: The sky is the limit.

M326: You can accomplish anything you want

to.

SS327: You will see when you cross that

bridge.

M327: When you come to that point in life

you will understand.

SS328: He or she is railroading you.

M328: He or she is taking advantage of you.

SS329: Do not throw the baby out with the

bathwater.

M329: Do not forget the real purpose

behind things.

SS330: Last kick at the bucket.

M330: Last chance at life to do what
you want to do.


SS331: He or she is like the wind.

M331: He or she is a person who comes and
goes out of peoples lives as they please.


SS332: It will be a barn burner.

M332: It will be a real party.


SS333: Read the fine print.

M333: Read the details of a contract.


SS334: Do not throw in the towel.

M334: Do not give up.

SS335: I broke up in stitches.

M335: I laughed so hard it hurt.


SS336: They were fighting like cats and dogs.

M336: They were really fighting hard.


SS337: Go down in flames

M337: Fail miserably


SS338: He or she is bubbly.

M338: He or she is fun to be around and
is always upbeat and outgoing.


SS339: He or she is a ray of sunshine.

M339: He or she brings life to everywhere
they go and are fun to be around.

SS340: Tongue tied

M340: Having trouble speaking

SS341: Stone face.

M341: An expressionless face.

SS342: Get off my case.

M342: Do not bother me and leave me alone.

SS343: Get off my back.

M343: Do not bother me and leave me alone.

SS344: When it rains it pours.

M344: When problems come in life,

they come all at the same time.

SS345: I am calling a spade a spade.

M345: The truth is the truth.


SS346: He or she lies through their teeth.

M346: He or she is good at lying and

do it often.


SS347: He or she is hot to trot.

M347: He or she is attractive.


SS348: Start from scratch.

M348: Start from the beginning with nothing

done so far.


SS349: He or she is full of shit

M349: He or she is a complete liar.

SS350: He or she is putting on a front.

M350: He or she is not being totally honest and transparent.

SS351: He or she is as cold as ice.

M351: A person who is not caring or has no personality.

SS352: You are just blowing your own horn.

M352: The person is just bragging

SS353: Comfortable in my own skin

M353: Comfortable with who you are

SS354: He or she is a rat.

M354: A person who tells about you when you are not there or present.

SS355: You are airing your dirty laundry.

M355: A person who talks about personal

information in public.

SS356: He or she has their head in the clouds.

M356: He or she thinks they are really

important when they are not.

SS357: He or she is talking behind your back.

M357: He or she is talking bad about you

when you are not there.

SS358: They run you into the ground.

M358: They insult you when you are not

there with no mercy shown.

SS359: He or she is an open book.

M359: He or she is transparent.


SS360: One door closed is another one

opened.

M360: An opportunity is disguise


SS361: The heat is on.

M361: The pressure is on.


SS362: If you cannot stand the heat then get

out of the kitchen

M362: If cannot stand the pressure of a

pressured environment then leave.

SS363: He or she wears their heart on their

   sleeves.

M363: He or she shows their emotions and

   feelings openly.

SS364: A bible thumper.

M364: A real religious person

SS365: He or she is hammered.

M365: He or she is drunk.

SS366: He or she is corked.

M366: He or she is drunk.

SS367: It is like mating elephants.

M367: A very difficult task to undertake.

SS368: He or she is a straight shooter.

M368: He or she is honest.


SS369: Stop on a dime.

M369: Stop precisely.


SS370: Everything is in there but the kitchen

sink.

M370: Everything is in there.


SS371: They lead you down the garden path.

M371: They promise you everything to give

you nothing.


SS372: I had it on the tip of my tongue

M372: I know what I was about to say and

forgot it

SS373: You are off the rails

M373: You are completely out of your mind


SS374: Madder than a wet hen

M374: Really mad


SS375: You are talking out of your ass

M375: They do not know what they are talking

about but they think they do


SS376: None of your bee's wax

M376: None of your business


SS377: If the shoe fits wear it

M377: If it suits you

SS378: Early bird gets the worm

M378: Early people get first selection or choice

SS379: Cool as a cucumber

M379: Really relaxed and poised person

SS380: Smooth as a baby's bottom

M380: Really smooth

SS381: You are a tool

M381: You are useless

SS382: They are a loose cannon

M382: They have a temper and could be unpredictable

SS383: You covered all the bases

M383: You did a complete job


SS384: You covered your ass

M384: You protected yourself


SS385: You are a klutz

M385: You are clumsy


SS386: You are in the dog house

M386: Usually refers to a man who has

offended


SS387: Beat around the bush

M387: To not be straight forward

SS388: A straight-laced person

M388: A serious and no fun person


SS389: Shake or break a leg

M389: Good luck


SS390: Three bricks short of a load

M390: Not too smart


SS391: Cutting corners

M391: Being cheap


SS392: It will backfire on them

M392: Their plan will not work out


SS393: Easy does it

M393: Slow down

SS394: You are my anchor

M394: You are my support


SS395: It is not rocket science

M395: It is not difficult to figure out


SS396: Wouldn't that rot your socks

M396: Unbelievable that happened


SS397: Get something out of your system

M397: Release yourself of a burden


SS398: A sandwich short of a picnic

M398: Not too smart


SS399: Keep my feet on the ground

M399: Stay stable and secure

SS400: The best of both worlds

M400: An ideal situation


SS401: Pull someone's leg

M401: To tell someone a joke


SS402: There is always a bigger fish

M402: There is someone always more

   important


SS403: Gone by the wayside

M403: Gone without ever getting it back


SS404: To get bent out of shape

M404: To get upset

SS405: Holding his own

M405: Taking care of themselves in a good

way

SS406: Your guess is as good as mine

M406: I have no idea

SS407: I will give you my 2 cents worth

M407: I will give you my opinion

SS408: Dodged a bullet

M408: Avoided a danger or a threat

SS409: You are a turkey

M409: You are a jokingly fool

SS410: You are a clown

M410: You are not a serious person


SS411: Off the cuff

M411: Without much thought


SS412: Educated bum

M412: An unemployed person with an education


SS413: You are a bum

M413: A no good or unemployed person


SS414: It is raining cats and dogs

M414: It is really raining hard


SS415: Pardon my French

M415: Excuse me for saying the wrong thing

SS416: Do not take it to heart

M416: Do not take it personally


SS417: Look at the bright side

M417: Be optimistic


SS418: Keep your chin up

M418: Do let things get to you and stay

positive


SS419: Grass is always greener on the other

side

M419: A person thinks it is better elsewhere


SS420: One step at a time

M420: Take it slow

SS421: Life is not a bowl of cherries

M421: Life is not easy


SS422: Hold your horses

M422: Slow down


SS423: Cannot teach an old dog new tricks

M423: Cannot teach an old person, new things


SS424: Keep a level head

M424: Be sensible


SS425: Excuse me for living

M425: Sorry for saying something


SS426: Do not put the cart before the horse

M426: Do not get ahead of yourself

SS427: I am toasty

M427: I am warm


SS428: I am wired

M428: I am full of energy


SS429: He or she is shifty

M429: A person you cannot trust


SS430: Cut from the same cloth

M430: You are the same


SS431: Things are looking up

M431: Things are looking good


SS432: It looks like you have your hands full

M432: Busy

SS433: Do not lose heart

M433: Do not give up


SS434: Make a killing

M434: Make lots of money


SS435: Watch your back

M435: Be careful


SS436: I got him on the payroll

M436: I have him working for me


SS437: All in

M437: Totally committed with everything I

    have

SS438: Bullheaded

M438: Stubborn


SS439: Trying to get them out of my head

M439: Trying not to think about them


SS440: You have the green light

M440: You can go ahead and do it


SS441: The red flags are there

M441: The warning signs are there


SS442: He or she is the cat's ass

M442: He or she is wonderful

SS443: You look like a million bucks

M443: You look really good like a million

dollars


SS444: Dressed to kill

M444: Dressed really good


SS445: Dressed to the nines

M445: Dressed really good


SS446: Do not sit on the fence

M446: Do not be undecided


SS447: Get off the fence

M447: Make a decision

SS448: Beef it up

M448: Add more to it


SS449: Clear the air

M449: Confess your grievances or

settle the challenge in a relationship

by talking openly about it


SS450: Come clean

M450: Confess your mistake or shortcomings


SS451: Are we on the same page

M451: Are we in agreement


SS452: Not all there

M452: Not a hundred percent mentally fit

SS453: Not with it

M453: Not hundred percent mentally capable


SS454: Money bags

M454: A person with a lot of money


SS455: Wiggle your way out

M455: Slide your way out


SS456: Hard as nails

M456: Tough


SS457: Do not give me lip

M457: Do not sass me


SS458: How do like them apples

M458: How do you like the situation

SS459: Feeling on top of the world

M459: Feeling good


SS460: It is no picnic

M460: No fun


SS461: He or she is a bad apple

M461: He or she is a bad person


SS462: Show your true colours

M462: Show who you really are


SS463: If looks could kill

M463: Bad or dirty look


SS464: Past the point of no return

M464: Cannot turn back

SS465: Do not gip me

M465: Do not cheat me


SS466: You are in the in crowd

M466: You are in the popular crowd


SS467: Money is the root of all evil

M467: Money does not make you happy


SS468: He or she is running around

M468: He or she is cheating on a mate


SS469: It is coming down to the wire

M469: It is coming to the near end


SS470: Take the high road

M470: Don't fight or argue

SS471: Gone with the wind

M471: Flew away


SS472: Flatter than a pancake

M472: Real thin


SS473: The wheels are in motion

M473: Things are moving


SS474: Pemeal bacon

M474: Canadian bacon


SS475: A doormat

M475: A person who gets taken advantage of


SS476: Walk tall

M476: Be proud

SS477: He or she walks with their head too

high

M477: A prideful person

SS478: He or she needs to get knocked down

M478: To humble a prideful person

SS479: There is more than meets the eye

M479: More to discover

SS480: Mark my word

M480: I am right

SS481: Two heads are better than one

M481: Two people's thoughts or minds

are better than one

SS482: Sourpuss

M482: Miserable


SS483: You are like an orangutan

M483: Wild person


SS484: Just rolling out of me

M484: Just coming out easy


SS485: Worth its weight in gold

M485: Valuable


SS486: Great minds think alike

M486: Two people who think alike


SS487: Blue in the face

M487: Upset

SS488: It is all one sided

M488: One person thinking only


SS489: I am getting brain drain

M489: Mentally fatigued


SS490: It is a whole new ball game

M490: Starting over and new beginning


SS491: Whatever will be will be

M491: Accept the situation, it is fate


SS492: Do not stick out your neck

M492: Do not get involved


SS493: Life is what you make it

M493: Make things happen

SS494: Hold your tongue

M494: Keep quiet


SS495: Watch your mouth

M495: Be careful what you say


SS496: Life is a seesaw

M496: Back and forth


SS497: You are milking it for all its worth

M497: You are getting as much value out
of something without much effort


SS498: There is no thing such as a free lunch

M498: Nothing is free, there is a catch to it

SS499: No dirt on him or her

M499: No gossip or bad things to

say about him or her


SS500: Fly the coup

M500: Take off and leave


SS501: A stitch in time saves nine

M501: Fix the problem now before it gets

worse


SS502: All decked out

M502: Dressed well or with all the extras


SS503: Roll out the red carpet

M503: Welcome people

SS504: Roll the dice

M504: Take a chance


SS505: Is that all there is?

M505: Disappointment


SS506: The glass is half full not half empty

M506: Be positive


SS507: It went over his head

M507: He did not understand or respond


SS508: Loaded question

M508: A question presented, if answered

will incriminate yourself

SS509: Kick it to the curb

M509: Put it out on the street to be

    taken away like garbage


SS510: Love triangle

M510: Two persons competing for the

    same love interest


SS511: Everything always happens in three's

M511: Good or bad events is believed

    to come one after another three times


SS512: A neat drink

M512: A straight alcoholic drink with no mix in

    it

SS513: Better late than never

M513: Better to show up late then never


SS514: Good bones

M514: Good structure


SS515: Dot your I's and cross your t's

M515: Do a complete job


SS516: Knee deep

M516: In the thick of the task


SS517: Slow as a snail

M517: Real slow


SS518: The boob tube

M518: The television

SS519: The more things change the more they

stay

M519: It all boils down to the same thing


SS520: Diamonds are forever

M520: Does not wear out


SS521: Bug eyed

M521: Bulging eyes


SS522: You are going to the dogs

M522: Not going anywhere, a lost cause


SS523: It had the biscuit

M523: It is worn out

SS524: Clean their clock

M524: Beat them


SS525: Put your foot in your mouth

M525: Be quiet


SS526: Ugly duckling

M526: Real ugly


SS527: Ball and chain

M527: Married and tied down


SS528: Wrinkled like a prune

M528: Very wrinkled


SS529: Keep off the sauce

M529: Quit drinking alcohol

SS530: Meal ticket

M530: A person being financially supported

      by another

SS531: Tightwad

M531: A person who holds onto their money

      and does not spend it

SS532: Eat like pigs at a trough

M532: To eat a lot

SS533: Pigging out

M533: Eating a lot

SS534: Being above board

M534: Being honest

SS535: New kid on the block

M535: New person


SS536: Like it or lump it

M536: Take it or leave it


SS537: You are the cat's meow

M537: You are really something


SS538: You are a bone-rack

M538: Skinny


SS539: Home is where you make it

M539: You can live anywhere and be comfortable


SS540: The big cheese

M540: The big boss

SS541: Three's a crowd

M541: One too many persons


SS542: I am drawing a line in the sand.

M542: Setting up your boundaries that cannot
be crossed, usually in personal
relationships.


SS543: You are a stick in the mud.

M543: You are not much fun to bring along.


SS544: It is a dead-end street.

M544: Not going anywhere good going in that
direction, usually referring to
opportunities that have no chance of
success.

SS545: Throw me a line.

M545: Help me out

SS546: You killed two birds with one stone.

M546: You accomplished two things with one

effort.

SS547: He or she is hot.

M547: He or she is really good looking or

attractive.

SS548: Gung Ho.

M548: All for it with maximum interest and

effort.

SS549: Are you big on.

M549: Are you interested in.

SS550: You need that like a hole in the head.

M550: You do not need that.


SS551: Rain on my parade.

M551: When I am having a good time or

celebration and you are trying to

bring me down and depress me.


SS552: It is through the roof.

M552: It is more than what we expected

or anticipated.


SS553: It is all smoke and mirrors.

M553: It is all lies and deceit.


SS554: It is crystal clear.

M554: It is really clear and obvious.

SS555:  Six feet under.

M555: Buried and dead.


SS556: New broom sweeps

M556: New manager or boss makes

new improvements or rules.


SS557: Swept under the bridge.

M557: Forgotten


SS558: Swept off of my feet.

M558: Usually refers to a person who is

overtaken by their initial love of

their life that surprises them.


SS559: Waste not, want not

M559: Do not waste things

SS560: A rock and a hard place.

M560: No place to go

SS561: Getting your juices flowing.

M561: Get going

SS562: Do not let the cat out of the bag.

M562: Do not reveal the secret.

SS563: The birds and the bees.

M563: Love and sex.

SS564: I was not born yesterday.

M564: I am not stupid.

SS565: Play it by ear.

M565: Improvise

SS566: A chip on my shoulder.

M566: Got a grudge

SS567: I have cold feet

M567: I am fearful

SS568: Out in left field.

M568: Not mentally fit

SS569: Not playing with a full deck.

M569: Not 100 percent mentally fit.

SS570: Silence is golden.

M570: Silence is very good and special.

SS571: Looks good on paper.

M571: Looks good written down but not

   verbally

SS572: Own it.

M572: Take responsibility for your actions.

SS573: Whitewashed

M573: Erased

SS574: Swept under the carpet

M574: Hidden from sight

SS575: Busy body

M575: Nosy person

SS576: It just flows

M576: It just comes together


SS577: Let bygones be bygones

M577: To forgive


SS578: Going concern

M578: Active person


SS579: You are pain in the butt or side

M579: A nuisance


SS580: Come rain or shine

M580: No matter what


SS581: Think outside the box

M581: Have a broader outlook on things

SS582: They are sweet as honey

M582: They are very sweet and nice


SS583: You cannot bank on it

M583: You cannot count on it


SS584: Strike the iron while it is hot

M584: Make a quick move


SS585: Put up or shut up

M585: Do it or do not do it


SS586: Clear as a bell

M586: Really clear


SS587: Loosen up

M587: Relax

SS588: It takes two to tango

M588: Where two people are involved both
    are responsible


SS589: You cannot have it both ways

M589: You cannot have everything


SS590: Right down to a science

M590: Figured it out completely


SS591: They are fighting like cats and dogs

M591: They are fighting intensely


SS592: You took the words right out of my
    mouth

M592: You read my mind

SS593: That song is stuck in my head

M593: I cannot think any further


SS594: You are stuck in my head

M594: I am thinking about you a lot


SS595: I cannot get you out of my head

M595: I cannot stop thinking about you


SS596: Near beer

M596: Non alcoholic beer


SS597: Water off your back

M597: Do not worry about it


SS598: Like a snake

M598: Sneaky

SS599: Weasel your way out

M599: Sneak your way out


SS600: Do not judge a book by its cover

M600: Do not judge by outward appearances


SS601: Holy Cow!

M601: I am surprised


SS602: Play the field

M602: Keep your options open and do not

commit to one person.


SS603: Cannot make heads or tail out of it

M603: Cannot come to a conclusion

SS604: My Hats off to you

M604: Congratulations


SS605: That is highway robbery

M605: Something being sold that is overpriced


SS606: Pull up your pants

M606: Get your act together


SS607: Roll up your sleeves

M607: Do what you have to do


SS608: Beggars cannot be choosers

M608: You are in no position to be picky or

selective

SS609: Step it up a notch

M609: Take things to a higher level


SS610: A notch in my belt

M610: An experience that you have now


SS611: Chill Out

M611: Just relax and take it easy


SS612: Baker's dozen

M612: Thirteen


SS613: Get out of my hair

M613: Leave me alone because you are

bothering me

SS614: You are getting under my skin

M614: You are bothering me


SS615: Do not get fresh with me

M615: Do not try to get intimate with me


SS616: Take the road less traveled

M616: Be a pioneer and do something new


SS617: I am getting things off my chest

M617: Opening up about what is bothering

you and letting it out to be released


SS618: You are on the wrong side of the fence

M618: You are on the bad side of life or a

situation

SS619: Bring home the bacon

M619: Bring home the money


SS620: I am back to, square one

M620: I am back to the beginning


SS621: Lost your marbles

M621: Gone crazy


SS622: Cute as a button

M622: Really cute


SS623: Back to the drawing board

M623: Back to the beginning of a job or

      project

SS624: Who woke up on the wrong side of the bed

M624: Someone who woke up not feeling good or irritable


SS625: Do not cry over spilt milk

M625: It is nothing to worry about


SS626: I have got your back

M626: I will support you no matter what


SS627: He or She is a looker

M627: He or She is good looking and attractive


SS628: Nothing to write home about

M628: Nothing that important

SS629: All on my shoulders

M629: The responsibility is all mine


SS630: A gold digger

M630: After a person for their money


SS631: He or She is in the same boat

M631: He or She is in the same circumstances

or situation


SS632: Fly by night

M632: A person who is not committed or to

be taken seriously


SS633: You live by the seat of your pants

M633: A person who lives irresponsibility and

takes chances

SS634: They want to keep you in the dark

M634: People who want to keep secrets and

not tell you the information you want

or need


SS635: You nailed it

M635: You did the task or said the

opinion really good


SS636: You hit the nail on the head

M636: You said the opinion or perspective

perfectly


SS637: I quit cold turkey

M637: I quit right away without any help

or products

SS638: They are a piece of work

M638: They have a lot of faults and

imperfections


SS639: If you play with fire you are going to

get burned

M639: If you keep tempting trouble it will

catch up with and you will get hurt


SS640: Love is blind

M640: Love is very powerful and can

make you overlook flaws


SS641: That is icing on the cake

M641: Perfect way to finish

SS642: Every cloud has a silver lining

M642: Every bad thing has something

good hidden in it


SS643: Do not count your chickens

before they hatch

M643: Do not sure of a thing until it has

happened


SS644: The golden rule

M644: Do unto others as you would have

them do to you


SS645: On cloud nine

M645: Very happy

SS646: Live and learn

M646: Made a mistake


SS647: Look before you leap

M647: Think before you take a chance


SS648: Once in a blue moon

M648: Rarely


SS649: Duking it out

M649: Fighting it out


SS650: Like a three-ring circus

M650: Out of control


SS651: Far fetched

M651: Stretch the truth

SS652: Coming back to bite you

M652: Something bad resurfacing


SS653: Birds eye view

M653: Wide open view


SS654: Few and far between

M654: Scarce


SS655: Let the show come to you

M655: Let people approach you


SS656: Couch potato

M656: Someone who likes to lie on the couch

      a lot

SS657: It is a walk in the park

M657: It is easy


SS658: Pie in the face

M658: Belittled


SS659: It places a toll on you

M659: It is hard on you


SS660: Grasping at straws

M660: Not enough evidence


SS661: Play devil's advocate

M661: Take the opposite position against

　　　someone

SS662: Put something on ice

M662: Put it on hold


SS663: Saving for a rainy day

M663: Saving for later


SS664: Spill the beans

M664: Let out a secret


SS665: Take a rain check

M665: Do it another time


SS666: The devil is in the details

M666: If you look deeper it Is not good


SS667: The ball is in your court

M667: It is your decision to make

SS668: Third time is a charm

M668: It usually works the third time

around


SS669: You two are an item

M669: You two are a new couple or are

just spending a lot of time together


SS670: I feel burnt

M670: Someone did me wrong


SS671: You are drying out

M671: You are staying away from alcohol after

consuming alcohol for some time

SS672: You cannot see the forest for the trees

M672: You cannot see the truth in front of
your face


SS673: You are a chicken

M673: You are a coward


SS674: You are looking in the rear-view
mirror too much.

M674: You are looking at your past
or past mistakes too much.


SS675: Look what the cat dragged in.

M675: Someone just come to you, and you
say this, because you did not expect
them to come at that time in that
condition.

SS676: Are you sold on that.

M676: Do you want that or are convinced

about that.


SS677: I am sold.

M677: I am convinced.


SS678: I have the t-shirt.

M678: I have experience in that


SS679: I will be by your side

M679: I will support you


SS680: The writing is on the wall.

M680: The truth that has always been there

is there for you to see

SS681: Heads up.

M681: Pay attention.


SS682: You are eating off my plate.

M682: You are taking from me what I need


SS683: Do you want to jump in the sack.

M683: Do you want to have sex.


SS684: Do you want to roll around in the hay.

M684: Do you want to have sex.


SS685: You have missed the boat.

M685: You have missed the opportunity.


SS686: It is as straight as a dime.

M686: It is really straight.

SS687: In there like a dirty shirt.

M687: Involved.


SS688: Let them off the hook.

M688: Let them get away from there

responsibilities.


SS689: Leave no stone unturned

M689: Look everywhere


SS690: An apple a day keeps the doctors away.

M690: Apples are good for you.


SS691: It is a dog eat; dog world.

M691: Every person has to survive in this

world by themselves.

SS692: You can take it to the bank.

M692: It is a sure thing and you can count on

it.

SS693: You are in the red.

M693: You are in debt.


SS694: This place is a zoo.

M694: This place is really busy.


SS695: What is cooking?

M695: What is happening with you.


SS696: He or she has a big mouth.

M696: He or she talks a lot or gossips a lot.

SS697: Put the pedal to the metal.

M697: Press the gas pedal down to the floor

to accelerate fast in a car or in life

SS698: This place is a gold mine.

M698: This place makes a lot of money.

SS699: You got horseshoes up your ass.

M699: You are really lucky.

SS700: You must have eaten your Wheaties.

M700: You have a lot of energy and

motivation.

SS701: You can run circles around him or her.

M701: You are more athletic.

SS702: You are stubborn as a mule.

M702: Very stubborn.


SS703: You are coarse as a horse.

M703: Very coarse.


SS704: I am running on empty.

M704: I have no energy.


SS705: Cry me a river.

M705: Cry as much as you can because

I do not care.


SS706: She is knocked up.

M706: She is pregnant.

SS707: Out of the frying pan and into the fire

M707: Things getting from bad to worse


SS708: Necessity is the mother of invention

M708: When you are forced to do something;

you will


SS709: It is what it is

M709: You cannot do anything about it


SS710: Do not shoot yourself in the foot

M710: Do set yourself up for failure


SS711: This place is a pig pen or pig sty

M711: This place is messy or dirty

SS712: They are damaged goods

M712: They emotionally unhealthy


SS713: I am stoned

M713: I am intoxicated or drunk or high


SS714: I am high

M714: I am on drugs


SS715: That went up in smoke

M715: That vanished or disappeared


SS716: That suits him or her to a tee

M716: That fits him or her perfectly


SS717: Nick Knacks

M717: Useful things

SS718: Out of sorts

M718: Not feeling too well


SS719: That is the last straw

M719:  That is the last time


SS720: It is like night and day

M720: The difference is clear and obvious


SS721: It is big of you

M721: It is generous of you


SS722: Life can change on a dime

M722: Life can change quickly


SS723: I have a hand on things

M723: I have control of things

SS724: Get a grip on things

M724: Get control of your things


SS725: Get a grip

M725: Get control of yourself


SS726: Wet your whistle

M726: Have a drink


SS727: Packed to the gills

M727: Packed full


SS728: It is a donkey's age

M728: It is a long time


SS729: A sad sack

M729: An unhappy person

SS730: Spreading like a wildfire

M730: It is moving very fast


SS731: It eats your heart out

M731: You hurt


SS732: Eat your heart out

M732: Have all you want


SS733: Get up to speed

M733: Get updated


SS734: I said my peace

M734: I said what I had to say


SS735: It came from the horse's mouth

M735: It came from an original source

SS736: Birds of the same feather flock

together

M736: Similar people associate with each

other

SS737: You got all your feathers in a ruffle

M737: You are offended and have your guard

up

SS738: A cold night in hell

M738: Never

SS739: When hell freezes over

M739: Never

SS740: You are a horse's ass

M740: Not a nice person

SS741: Nose to nose

M741: Very close


SS742: A rolling stone gathers no moss

M742: Keep in motion and your life will be

fine


SS743: Roll with the punches

M743: Take what comes


SS744: Scot free

M744: Easily


SS745: Tow the line

M745: Behave

SS746: Ghost of a chance

M746: Not much of a chance

SS747: Weight lifted off of your shoulders

M747: A burden or stress lifted off of you

SS748: Getting pretty tight

M748: Getting close

SS749: It will come back to haunt you

M749: You will regret it

SS750: Sly as a fox

M750: Sneaky

SS751: Like banging your head against the wall

M751: Not getting anywhere

SS752: Dolled up

M752: Made beautiful


SS753: Bloated like a pig

M753: Ate too much


SS754: Mind over matter

M754: You can do it


SS755: Eye sore

M755: Not nice to look at


SS756: It is like finding a needle in a haystack

M756: Nearly impossible to find


SS757: Sober as a judge

M757: Really sober

SS758: Higher than a kite

M758: Really high or stoned or intoxicated


SS759: Selling like hot cakes

M759: Really popular and selling fast


SS760: Lickity Split

M760: Moving fast


SS761: Rough around the edges

M761: Not polished but rough


SS762: Keep plugging away

M762: Keep working at it


SS763: Are you plugged in

M763: Are you paying attention or interested

SS764: He is off his rocker

M764: He is crazy


SS765: Blow them out of the water

M765: Really shock or gain their attention


SS766: Rat race

M766: Busy society going to work and

       competing with each other


SS767: Bring it up to par

M767: Bring up to proper standards


SS768: Fortune favours the bold

M768: Take risks

SS769: There are other fish in the sea

M769: There are more potential partners out

there


SS770: There is no time like the present

M770: Do things now


SS771: Kick the bucket

M771: To die


SS772: The pot calling the kettle black

M772: Someone criticizing someone who is

just as bad


SS773: We see eye to eye

M773: We agree

SS774: There are clouds on the horizon

M774: There is trouble coming


SS775: Through thick and thin

M775: Through good and bad times


SS776: Time is money

M776: Work quickly


SS777: Weather the storm

M777: Go through something difficult


SS778: Run like the wind

M778: Run fast

SS779: Once bitten, twice shy

M779: Once you have been hurt you become

more cautious


SS780: Shape up or ship out

M780: Work better or leave


SS781: You are getting pickled

M781: You are getting drunk


SS782: Loonie

M782: A Canadian dollar coin


SS783: Toonie

M783: A Canadian two dollar coin

SS784: You can buy it for a song

M784: You can get it cheap


SS785: That person is sawing a log

M785: That person is sleeping and snoring


SS786: A Caesar

M786: A bloody Mary alcoholic drink with

vodka and clamato juice


SS787: A Mickey

M787: A small bottle of liquor


SS788: Pull the wool over your eyes

M788: Trying to fool or deceive you

SS789: You cannot change a leopard's spots

M789: You cannot change the way a person is


SS790: You cannot change a zebra's stripes

M790: You cannot change the way a person is


SS791: I feel sick to my stomach

M791: Feeling eery or ill


SS792: KD

M792: Kraft Dinner


SS793: He or she undressed them

M793: Made them look silly or foolish


SS794: Going to town on that

M794: Really working on that

SS795: He or she struck a chord with them

M795: Found something in common or
resonated with them


SS796: He or she talked down to me

M796: Belittled me


SS797: They run as fast as a cheetah

M797: They run very fast


SS798: They lie like a trooper

M798: They lie a lot


SS799: Bend over backwards for you

M799: Do anything for you

SS800: Cut the cheese

M800: Farted

SS801: Take a load of your mind

M801: Just relax and do not think about anything

SS802: Save face

M802: To reconcile

SS803: Toque

M803: A knitted winter cap

SS804: Cut it out

M804: Stop it

SS805: Clean as a whistle

M805: Very clean

SS806: Sparkling clean

M806: Shiny clean


SS807: Bone dry

M807: Very dry


SS808: You are a knight in shining armour

M808: You are a hero


SS809: Clean the table

M809: Sinking all of your balls playing billiards


SS810: A wallflower

M810: Nobody notices you


SS811: Good as gold

M811: Perfect and a sure thing

SS812: Life is not a storybook

M812: Life is real


SS813: I do not give a rat's ass

M813: I do not care


SS814: Happy go lucky

M814: Carefree


SS815: Glowing like a lightbulb

M815: Radiant


SS816: Bright eyed and bushy-tailed

M816: Alert


SS817: A big bag of wind

M817: Full of exaggeration

SS818: Time will tell

M818: The future will be known when it

comes

SS819: I have a bigger fish to fry

M819: I have a more important person

to take care of

SS820: Got wind of something

M820: Hear something you should not have

heard

SS821: You have to wake up pretty early in the

morning to get one by me

M821: I am not outsmarted easily

SS822: What is the score

M822: What is going on or what is the update


SS823: You can say that again

M823: It is true and I agree


SS824: Tickled pink

M824: Very pleased


SS825: An ounce of prevention is worth a
pound of cure

M825: Preventing illness or problems are
easier then trying to fix them later


SS826: White as snow

M826: Very white

SS827: The apple does not fall far from the

tree

M827: You are like your parents


SS828: Dumb as a rock

M828: Really dumb


SS829: Fit as a fiddle

M829: Really fit


SS830: It is a homerun

M830: It is a success


SS831: Nuttier than a fruitcake

M831: Real crazy

SS832: Clean as a whistle

M832: Real clean


SS833: I am so hungry I could eat a horse

M833: I am really hungry


SS834: Cheapskate

M834: A real financially frugal person


SS835: In the other person's pockets

M835: Someone who has mutual financial

interests with another


SS836: Here is the moment of truth

M836: Get to know what is going on

SS837: I just had a brainwave

M837: I just had a collection of thoughts or
ideas


SS838: Deep pockets

M838: Someone who holds on to their money


SS839: Proof is in the pudding

M839: Proof is in the evidence


SS840: You did the job half assed

M840: You did the job half good and half not
good

SS841: Cabin fever

M841: Feeling closed in and isolated from

being inside usually in the winter

season


SS842: You are a goodie two shoes

M842: Someone who thinks they are

wonderful


SS843: Were you born in a barn

M843: Someone who leaves the door open


SS844: Four eyes

M844: Usually someone wearing glasses


SS845: The idiot box

M845: The television

SS846: Skinny as a rake

M846: Real skinny


SS847: His or her bark is bigger than his

or her bite

M847: He or she makes a lot of noise but

no real threat

SS848: Absence makes the heart grow fonder

M848: Love grows when two people are apart


SS849: What is meant to be will be

M849: Inevitable


SS850: Hotter than a firecracker

M850: Real hot

SS851: Dirt cheap

M851: Real inexpensive, a good bargain


SS852: Going on a wild good chase

M852: Searching all over for something


SS853: Blind as a bat

M853: Real blind


SS854: Old as the hills

M854: Real old


SS855: Balder than a billiard ball

M855: Real bald


SS856: Balder than a bald eagle

M856: Real bald

SS857: Ugly as a bear

M857: Real ugly


SS858: You are getting ugly

M858: You are getting angry


SS859: Squeaky clean

M859: Real clean


SS860: I have a sweet tooth

M860: A person who likes candy or desserts


SS861: I am going squirrely

M861: I am going crazy


SS862: I am losing my mind

M862: I am going crazy

SS863: Carved in stone

M863: Something written or done that is

permanent


SS864: It is good do not knock it

M864: It is good and you should try it


SS865: No man is an island to himself

M865: Everyman has been influenced by

others


SS866: Go out with a bang

M866: Ending in victory


SS867: Do not bug me

M867: Do not bother me

SS868: Deader than a doorknob

M868: Real dead


SS869: To each his own

M869: Your own individual taste and choice


SS870: Get cracking

M870: Get moving


SS871: Blows my mind

M871: Unbelievable and overwhelming


SS872: Not missing a trick

M872: Not missing anything


SS873: Top of the line

M873: The best

SS874: Slow but surely wins the race

M874: Take your time and your will

end up the winner


SS875: That road goes nowhere

M875: No opportunities in that direction


SS876: Double dip

M876: Do not take just one but two


SS877: I got it on the hook

M877: I am doing it


SS878: They are on the clock

M878: They are being calculated for time

SS879: Avoid them like the black plague

M879: Avoid them at all costs


SS880: Hook, line and sinker

M880: You really believed in something

that was not true


SS881: You fell for it

M881: You believed in something that was not

true


SS882: Don't be a worry wart

M882: Don't worry so much


SS883: Do not want to upset the applecart

M883: Do not want to upset a stable situation

that could change if provoked

SS884: I am in the running

M884: I am in line


SS885: Stiffer than a board

M885: Uptight


SS886: Hanging on by a thread

M886: Near the edge


SS887: Thick skin

M887: You cannot get through to them


SS888: Thick as thieves

M888: People stick together


SS889. Call it a day

M889: Finish what you are doing

SS890: Get it while it is going-good

M890: Accept it now


SS891: Get it lean and mean

M891: Skimpy


SS892: Put your money where your mouth is

M892: Prove it


SS893: Talk is cheap

M893: Prove it


SS894: He or she is too big for their britches

M894: He or she thinks they are more

       important

SS895: Speak of the devil

M895: The person enters we were just talking

about

SS896: Do not give up your day job

M896: You are not good at what you are doing

SS897: Get a taste of your own medicine

M897: You got mistreated back to you

SS898: Ignorance is bliss

M898: You are better not knowing

SS899: It takes one to know one

M899: You are just as bad as me

SS900: Get out of town

M900: I do not believe you


SS901: You got rocks in your head

M901: Not thinking straight


SS902: Do something at a drop of a hat

M902: Do something spontaneously


SS903: Give someone the cold shoulder

M903: Ignore someone


SS904: Good things come to those who wait

M904: Be patient


SS905: Costs an arm and a leg

M905: Very expensive

SS906: What goes around comes around

M906: What you do to others they will do to you


SS907: They have a personality like a plant

M907: No personality


SS908: Loose as a goose

M908: Relaxed


SS909: Slow as a turtle

M909: Very slow


SS910: Karma is a bitch

M910: What bad you put out has come back to

to you

SS911: Tight as a drum

M911: A cheap or frugal person


SS912: The door swings both ways

M912: Give and take


SS913: Faster than a speeding bullet

M913: Really fast


SS914: It is the real deal

M914: It is legitimate


SS915: It is child's play

M915: It is easy and do not worry about it


SS916: Do not sugar coat it

M916: Give me the facts and truth

SS917: As the crow fly's

M917: Straight


SS918: On the gravy train

M918: Lots of benefits


SS919: The pickings are slim

M919: Not too much to choose from


SS920: Fast as lightening

M920: Real fast and speedy


SS921: Working like a slave

M921: Working hard


SS922: Tail between your legs

M922: Ashamed

SS923: Keeping a low profile

M923: Not socializing and hiding out


SS924: Laying low

M924: Not socializing and hiding out


SS925: Bottom drops out

M925: End of things


SS926: Run like a race horse

M926: Fast


SS927: Do you have plastic

M927: Do you have a credit card


SS928: Sharp as a razor

M928: Smart or extremely sharp

SS929: Red as a beet

M929: Very rosy


SS930: Hard as a rock

M930: Very hard


SS931: Growing like a weed

M931: Tall


SS932: Good as gold

M932: Nice


SS933: Swim like a fish

M933: Good swimmer


SS934: Wrap it up

M934: Finish it

SS935: Something is fishy

M935: Something is not right


SS936: Like a kid in a candy store

M936: Excited


SS937: Cannot hold a candle to him

M937: Cannot compete


SS938: That filled the gap

M938: I'm full of food


SS939: Sick as a dog

M939: Really sick


SS940: Bleed like a stuffed pig

M940: Blood flowing

SS941: Skeletons in the closet

M941: The hidden bad past


SS942: Coming out

M942: Declaring in public


SS943: Slam dunk

M943: Success


SS944: The pen is mightier than the sword

M944: Diplomacy is more influential


SS945: Get out of town

M945: I do not believe you


SS946: The motor purrs like a kitten

M946: Smooth or quiet engine

SS947: You got schooled

M947: You were taught a life lesson


SS948: Turn the other cheek

M948: Forgive


SS949: Time flies

M949: Time goes quickly


SS950: Take two

M950: Do it again a second time


SS951: Bump in the log

M951: Interruption


SS952: You have the munchies

M952: Hungry for snacks

SS953: Shaking like a leaf

M953: Shaking a lot


SS954: It is a piece of cake

M954: It is easy


SS955: Get your act together

M955: Get moving


SS956: Not to shabby

M956: Not to bad


SS957: Where there is a will there is a way

M957: You can always find your way


SS958: Practice makes perfect

M958: Keep at it and you will be good

SS959: Practice what you preach

M959: Do what you tell others to do


SS960: If the shoe fits let them wear it

M960: Let people be who they are


SS961: Do not be wise in your own eyes

M961: Do not view yourself as too smart


SS962: Bet your bottom dollar

M962: Sure thing


SS963: Talk to the wall

M963: I am not listening


SS964: Get your head on straight

M964: Think purposefully and clearly

SS965: Going number one

M965: Going pee


SS966: Going number two

M966: Going pooh


SS967: I am regular

M967: I have no trouble going number two


SS968: Sour grapes

M968: Bitter person


SS969: The ceiling is closing in on me

M969: I am being smothered


SS970: Take them for a ride

M970: Take advantage

SS971: I have got their number

M971: I know what they are about


SS972: Slept like a log

M972: Slept really well and deep


SS973: That is not my forte

M973: That is not my thing or interest


SS974: To the naked eye

M974: It is plain to see


SS975: The night is young

M975: A lot of time to have fun


SS976: That takes the cake

M976: That is unbelievable that happened

SS977: Living on pins and needles

M977: Living on edge


SS978: The elephant in the room

M978: The issue people are not talking about


SS979: Look where it is coming from

M979: The source of the ill will is happening

because they are no good


SS980: Time well spent

M980: Good use of your time


SS981: I beat you to the punch

M981: I beat you to the conclusion

SS982: Spot on

M982: Perfect


SS983: The bush

M983: Dense unpopulated forest


SS984: Milk it for all its worth

M984: Get as much as you can


SS985: It cuts like a knife

M985: An emotional injury like a physical one


SS986: Shake a leg

M986: Have fun and do the best you can


SS987: Busy as a bee

M987: Very busy

SS988: You got it made in the shade

M988: You got it good


SS989: Hindsight is 20/20

M989: Clear outlook


SS990: Play them like a fiddle

M990: Manipulate others


SS991: Not my cup of tea

M991: Not my personal preference


SS992: They have a spring in their step

M992: They are full of energy and life


SS993: Wheeling and dealing

M993: Make a bargain

SS994: Wheeler dealer

M994: A person who bargains


SS995: Burn bridges

M995: Ending relationships permanently


SS996: Keep the wheels turning

M996: Keep thinking


SS997: Ugly as a hedge fence

M997: Real ugly


SS998: Killing time

M998: Doing nothing


SS999: Putting the day in

M999: Killing time

SS1000: Dumb as a post

M1000: Real dumb


SS1001: That is old hat

M1001: That is old fashioned


SS1002: It is not up my alley

M1002: Does not interest me


SS1003: Ride the waves

M1003: Take the ups and downs


SS1004: Go with the flow

M1004: Go along with it


SS1005: Hang loose

M1005: Relax

SS1006: Get off your high horse

M1006: Do not be snobbish


SS1007: Weak as a kitten

M1007: Very weak


SS1008: Calm before the storm

M1008: Stability and quietness before

something bad is going to happen


SS1009: Been around the block

M1009: Have experience


SS1010: It is so quiet you can hear a pin drop

M1010: Very quiet

SS1011: You can lead a horse to water, but
you cannot make him drink

M1011: You can lead someone in the right
direction, but you cannot make them
do what is right

SS1012: Tied to your mother's apron strings

M1012: A boy who is close to and dependent
on their mother

SS1013: Mama's boy

M1013: A boy who is close to and dependent
on their mother

SS1014: It is a witch hunt

M1014: Out to get someone in a bad way

SS1015: It is a lost cause

M1015: It is a waste of time


SS1016: Time repeats itself

M1016: The same thing over and over


SS1017: Eating out of a box

M1017: Eating frozen dinners


SS1018: Television dinners

M1018: Pre-made microwaveable frozen

dinners


SS1019 Got the meat of it

M1019: Got the most of it

SS1020: A slice of humble pie

M1020: To be humbled partly


SS1021: Beach bum

M1021: Someone who hangs out at the beach

a lot


SS1022: Poutine

M1022: Fries, gravy and cheese curds


SS1023: Hung out to dry

M1023: Someone left you alone by yourself

without any support


SS1024: Cool your jets

M1024: Calm down

SS1025: Blessing in disguise

M1025: A blessing coming out to you

unexpectantly through something else

SS1026: They are a snowflake

M1026: They are crazy

SS1027: Eyes are the window of the soul

M1027: A person's eyes reveals who they

really are deep down inside

SS1028: You are fishing in the wrong pond

M1028: Looking in the wrong place for what

you want

SS1029: A Shrink

M1029: A Psychiatrist

SS1030: Nuke it

M1030: Microwave it


SS1031: A penny saved is a penny earned

M1031: It is good to save money


SS1032: Digging for dirt

M1032: A person looking for fault or

wrongdoing


SS1033: A penny pincher

M1033: Someone who is very frugal with there

money


SS1034: You are a pilon

M1034: Someone who stands or gets in the

way and does not move

SS1035: School of hard knocks

M1035: Life's experiences


SS1036: Smart as a whip

M1036: Pretty smart


SS1037: Pretty as a picture

M1037: Very beautiful


SS1038: Free as a bird

M1038: Real free


SS1039: The circle of life

M1039: You are born and then you die


SS1040: Life has come full circle

M1040: Back to where you started from

SS1041: That hit the spot

M1041: Just what I needed


SS1042: Familiarity breeds contempt

M1042: Being around a person a lot you

end up liking them less


SS1043: They wear the pants in the family

M1043: They are the boss in the family


SS1044: Do not drag me through the mud

M1044: Do not put me through a lot of

troubles


SS1045: One bird in one hand is better

than two in the bush

M1045: Do not be greedy

SS1046: Thick as thieves

M1046: So many


SS1047: You got to play the cards dealt to you

M1047: Work with whatever life gives you


SS1048: Do not be a stick in the mud

M1048: Boring person


SS1049: Whatever tickles your fancy

M1049: Whatever you desire


SS1050: Do not be a stickler

M1050: Do not be in the way


SS1051: Do not be a poor sport

M1051: Do not be a sore loser

SS1052: Do not be a sore loser

M1052: Do not be upset with a situation


SS1053: Here is a penny for your thoughts

M1053: Let me know what you think


SS1054: Smart ass

M1054: Silly


SS1055: Smarty pants

M1055: Thinks their keen


SS1056: Pull a fast one

M1056: Manipulate


SS1057: Pull one over on me

M1057: Try to use me

SS1058: Off the top of your head

M1058: Without thinking


SS1059: Back to the grindstone

M1059: Back to work


SS1060: Put on your thinking cap

M1060: Use your brain


SS1061: All the bells and whistles

M1061: Comes with everything


SS1062: Our relationship is on the rocks

M1062: Not a steady and stable relationship


SS1063: Dapper Dan

M1063: Slick person

SS1064: You are a quack

M1064: You are crazy


SS1065: Where there is smoke there is fire

M1065: Expect the worst


SS1066: He or she dropped a bombshell

M1066: It has been exposed


SS1067: That is a thing of the past

M1067: Out of date


SS1068: Hold the fort

M1068: Look after things


SS1069: Phony as a three-dollar bill

M1069: Not valid

SS1070: Big as a whale

M1070: Huge


SS1071: If your number is up

M1071: It is meant to be


SS1072: You are pie eyed

M1072: You are drunk


SS1073: Join the ranks

M1073: Get in line


SS1074: That is in a nutshell

M1074: That is complete


SS1075: Your writing is like hen scratching

M1075: Writing that is messy and unclear

SS1076: Shop till you drop

M1076: Do not give up


SS1077: Light as a feather

M1077: Extremely light


SS1078: Barking up the wrong tree

M1078: Asking for trouble


SS1079: Run out of gas

M1079: Run out of energy


SS1080 The long and short story of it

M1080: That is the story of it


SS1081: Turn over a new leaf

M1081: Start a new change in your life

SS1082: It is getting pretty thin

M1082: Not much left


SS1083: No rest for the wicked

M1083: No peace of mind for evil people


SS1084: Neat freak

M1084: Real tidy person


SS1085: Speed demon

M1085: Fast driver


SS1086: You are having a hay day

M1086: Having fun


SS1087: Two peas in a pod

M1087: Alike

SS1088: Two faced person

M1088: Not a sincere person


SS1089: Lie with a straight face

M1089: Good liar with no guilt


SS1090: Beauty is only skin deep

M1090: Superficial


SS1091: Take them to the cleaners

M1091: Take what they have


SS1092: Do not fence me in

M1092: Do not confine me


SS1093: Happy as a lark

M1093: Very happy

SS1094: Got the world by the tail

M1094: Have success

SS1095: Life is full of ups and downs

M1095: Life is like a rollercoaster

SS1096: People who live in glass houses

should not throw stones

M1096: Do not judge others

SS1097: You cannot make an omelet

unless you break some eggs

M1097: Everything has a cost to it

SS1098: You are full of beans

M1098: Not truthful

SS1099: Going to beat the band

M1099: Going fast


SS1100: Get the ball rolling

M1100: Start moving


SS1101: Stuffed shirt

M1101: Rigid stiff person


SS1102: You are swamped

M1102: You are overworked


SS1103: Hang up your spurs

M1103: Retire


SS1104: You are a push over

M1104: Easy to control

SS1105: Work your fingers to the bone

M1105: Working hard


SS1106: Sitting on the John

M1106: Sitting on the toilet


SS1107: King of the castle

M1107: Leader


SS1108: You made your bed now you have to

lie in it

M1108: Face consequences of your actions


SS1109: Life is a merry go round

M1109: Over and over

SS1110: Get a handle on it

M1110: Get control of it


SS1111: Sowing your wild oats

M1111: Experiencing promiscuous sex


SS1112: Take it to a higher level

M1112: Move on up


SS1113: No pain and no gain

M1113: You have to work for what you want


SS1114: So far so good

M1114: Things are going good so far


SS1115: Wrap you head around that

M1115: Understand something difficult

SS1116: A picture is worth a thousand words

M1116: Better to show then tell


SS1117: Bite off more than you can chew

M1117: Doing something that is too much to

       do


SS1118: By the skin of your teeth

M1118: Just barely


SS1119: Actions speak louder than words

M1119: Believe what people do not what they say


SS1120: Add insult to injury

M1120: Make a situation worse

SS1121: Comparing apples to oranges

M1121: Two things that cannot be compared

SS1122: Go on a wild goose chase

M1122: To do something that has no end

SS1123: Do not put all your eggs in one basket

M1123: Diversify your options to stay safe

SS1124: A stone's throw away

M1124: Not far

SS1125: Jack of all trades

M1125: A handyman

SS1126: Touch wood

M1126: Hope it comes true

SS1127: Road kill

M1127: Dead animal on the road


SS1128: You have been railroaded

M1128: You have been pushed aside


SS1129: Queen of Sheeba

M1129: Somebody special


SS1130: Smart cookie

M1130: Brilliant person


SS1131: Smart Alec

M1131: Sarcastic person


SS1132: He or she is spiffy

M1132: He or she looks good

SS1133: You sing like a canary

M1133: A person who mouths off

or squeals confident information


SS1134: God speed

M1134: Good luck on your way


SS1135: Run at the mouth

M1135: A mouthy person


SS1136: It is in dog years

M1136: A short time


SS1137: Spice of life

M1137: Enjoyable

SS1138: Prince charming

M1138: Handsome


SS1139: I do not know you from an ant

to a mole in the hill

M1139: Not familiar with you


SS1140: I do not know you from Adam

M1140: Not familiar with you


SS1141: A drop in the bucket

M1141: Very little


SS1142: Baby face

M1142: Young looking

SS1143: Got a handle on it

M1143: Got a grip on it


SS1144: Give me a drink on the rocks

M1144: A drink with ice cubes


SS1145: Bust your chops

M1145: Get working


SS1146: A fairy-tale wedding

M1146: A perfect wedding


SS1147: Look at life through rose coloured

   glasses

M1147: Life is not perfect

SS1148: Thrown under the bus

M1148: Put someone down


SS1149: Double down

M1149: Really go to work


SS1150: Do not go out on a limb

M1150: Do not take a chance


SS1151: Lay it on thick

M1151: Exaggerate


SS1152: Second wind

M1152: Strength to go ahead again


SS1153: Lots to crow about

M1153: A lot to complain about

SS1154: Curiosity killed the cat

M1154: Do not be nosy


SS1155: Got a monkey on your back

M1155: Something holding you back


SS1156: No rhyme or reason

M1156: No answer


SS1157: Squeaky wheel gets the grease

M1157: Those who complain get the most
attention


SS1158: Down and out

M1158: You do not have anything going for
you

SS1159: Going to get some rays

M1159: Going to get some sunshine


SS1160: Do not fiddle around

M1160: Do not play with it


SS1161: Do not horse around

M1161: Be careful


SS1162: Do not clown around

M1162: Be careful


SS1163: Slow as molasses

M1163: Very slow


SS1164: Hot as a pistol

M1164: Very hot

SS1165: Beauty is in the eye of the beholder

M1165: Depends of a person's tastes or

preference

SS1166: Quiet as a mouse

M1166: Very quiet

SS1167: Smooth as glass

M1167: Extremely smooth

SS1168: Mud in your eye

M1168: Got blinded by it

SS1169: Sly as a snake

M1169: Sneaky

SS1170: Walking on eggshells

M1170: Living on edge


SS1171: Treading on thin ice

M1171: Taking a chance


SS1172: White as a ghost

M1172: Pale


SS1173: By the book

M1173: Stick to the rules


SS1174: It will come out in the wash

M1174: The truth will come out eventually

SS1175: You cannot have your cake and eat it
too

M1175: You cannot have it both ways

SS1176: Grew up on the wrong side of the
tracks

M1176: Bad person

SS1177: Crocodile tears

M1177: Big tears

SS1178: That one really got his goat

M1178: Upset

SS1179: Drinks like a fish

M1179: Drinks a lot of alcohol

SS1180: Justice is served

M1180: The end is here or final verdict


SS1181: Mind your business

M1181: Don't be nosy


SS1182: Brain drain

M1182: Cannot think


SS1183: Beat you to the draw

M1183: Nobody's going to get there first


SS1184: It is second nature

M1184: Comes naturally


SS1185: Put a sock in it

M1185: Shut up and be quiet

SS1186: I am feeling blue

M1186: I am feeling depressed


SS1187: I am feeling under the weather

M1187: I am feeling sick


SS1188: I don't bite

M1188: I am harmless


SS1189: You eat like a truck driver

M1189: Big eater


SS1190: That leaves a bad taste in your mouth

M1190: That does not feel right


SS1191: Pulling your leg

M1191: Kidding you

SS1192: Bluffing

M1192: Lying


SS1193: Up and down like a yo-yo

M1193: All over the place


SS1194: Up in smoke

M1194: Vanished


SS1195: That ship has sailed

M1195: It is over and done with


SS1196: Try walking in my shoes

M1196: See what it is like to be me


SS1197: Go and bake a cake

M1197: Get lost

SS1198: Motoring along

M1198: Cruising along


SS1199: It is not all a bunch of roses

M1199: It is not all perfect


SS1200: Consider it a write off

M1200: End of it or a loss


SS1201: On the warpath

M1201: Upset


SS1202: Face the music

M1202: Take what is coming to you


SS1203: Read between the lines

M1203: Come to a conclusion

SS1204: On the ball

M1204: With it


SS1205: To die for

M1205: To really like it


SS1206: Give me a break

M1206: Be nice to me


SS1207: Rack my brains

M1207: Thinking hard


SS1208: On a roll

M1208: Winning streak


SS1209: Run into a few speedbumps

M1209: To hold you back

SS1210: Run into a few hurdles

M1210: Come across a few restrictions

   or obstructions


SS1211: Crunch the numbers

M1211: Calculate the numbers


SS1212: I will sit on it

M1212: I will think about it


SS1213: Short and sweet

M1213: Get it over with


SS1214: Right off the wall

M1214: Not with it

SS1215: Take you for a drive

M1215: Get rid of you


SS1216: Let's get this show on the road

M1216: Get moving


SS1217: You are cut off

M1217: No more for you


SS1218: It is curtains for you

M1218: You are done


SS1219: Brain dead

M1219: Cannot think or stupid person


SS1220: Final nail in the coffin

M1220: The end of it is here

SS1221: Pull a fast one

M1221: To deceive


SS1222: Pull one over on me

M1222: To deceive


SS1223: Pull one over on my eyes

M1223: To deceive


SS1224: Smart ass

M1224: Sarcastic


SS1225: Throw in the towel

M1225: To give up


SS1226: Redneck

M1226: An unpolished country or rural person

SS1227: Got a charge out of it

M1227: Got excited


SS1228: Car is a lemon

M1228: Unreliable car, usually made that way


SS1229: Top of my head

M1229: Without much thought


SS1230: Right up my alley

M1230: Just what I like


SS1231: The shit hit the fan

M1231: Things happened


SS1232: Dumb as a rock

M1232: Not smart

SS1233: In one ear and out the other

M1233: You are not listening


SS1234: Jump on the bandwagon

M1234: Ready to go for it and follow

what is popular


SS1235: Off the wagon

M1235: Not drinking alcohol anymore


SS1236: I have been skunked

M1236: I have been beat badly


SS1237: It would go over

M1237: It would be accepted or succeed

SS1238: I am at the end of my rope

M1238: You have come to the end


SS1239: You are a breath of fresh air

M1239: You are new and exciting


SS1240: You are a barrel of laughs

M1240: You are funny


SS1241: You have got time on your hands

M1241: You have time to spare


SS1242: We are on a roll

M1242: We are moving along


SS1243: Life is a breeze

M1243: Life is easy

SS1244: It is like taking candy from a baby

M1244: It is easy to get


SS1245: The train stops here

M1245: It is over


SS1246: The train has left the station

M1246: It is too late


SS1247: Step up to the plate

M1247: Take responsibility


SS1248: Feeling on top of the world

M1248: Feeling great


SS1249: Reach for the stars

M1249: Aim high

SS1250: Melt down

M1250: A bad day


SS1251: Full of wind

M1251:  Exaggerating the truth


SS1252: Full of hot air

M1252: A person who brags or exaggerates


SS1253: Ugly as sin

M1253: Very ugly


SS1254: Seeing life in colour

M1254: Seeing everything


SS1255: Fighting tooth and nail

M1255: Fighting with everything you got

SS1256: One track mind

M1256: Narrow thinking


SS1257: What a whiz

M1257: A smart person


SS1258: Not up to par

M1258: Not up to expectations


SS1259: Brainwashed

M1259: Taught to think a certain way


SS1260: Got skunked

M1260: You lost badly


SS1261: Funnier than a barrel of monkeys

M1261: Very funny

SS1262: Drunker than a skunk

M1262: Very drunk


SS1263: Bored stiff

M1263: Very bored


SS1264: Holy moly!

M1264: Wow!


SS1265: Finger in the eye

M1265: You cannot see


SS1266: Axe to grind

M1266: Grudge against a person


SS1267: He or she will have a bird

M1267: He or she will be shocked

SS1268: Shot in the dark

M1268: A chance


SS1269: Leader of the pack

M1269: Head chief


SS1270: He or She is out of your league

M1270: He or She is too good or too

good looking for you


SS1271: Coming out of the woodwork

M1271: Coming forth


SS1272: See the light of day

M1272: I saw my way

SS1273: Trial and error

M1273: Testing


SS1274: At lager-heads

M1274: Tied


SS1275: Sore back like a toothache

M1275: Very sore back


SS1276: Take time out

M1276: Have a break


SS1277: Keep a stiff upper lip

M1277: Be strong


SS1278: Keep your chin up

M1278: Be strong

SS1279: You must have broken her heart

M1279: You have over did it


SS1280: You are an air head

M1280: A dense person


SS1281: Mosy along

M1281: Move it along


SS1282: I am hooked

M1282: I am dependent or addicted


SS1283: Your eyes are bigger than your
stomach

M1283: You think you can eat more than
you can handle

SS1284: It is like watching paint dry

M1284: Very long and boring


SS1285: You are too far gone

M1285: You are beyond help


SS1286: Hell or highwater

M1286: Do it no matter what


SS1287: He or she has a short fuse

M1287: He or she has a temper


SS1288: Go jump in a lake

M1288: Get lost


SS1289: Gun shy

M1289: Afraid of commitment

SS1290: Two four

M1290: Twenty-four bottles of beer


SS1291: Timmies

M1291: Tim Hortons coffee shop


SS1292: Double-Double (coffee at Tim

Hortons)

M1292: Two creams and two sugars


SS1293: Regular (coffee at Tim Hortons)

M1293: One cream and one sugar


SS1294: Triple-Triple (coffee at Tim Hortons)

M1294: Three creams and three sugars

SS1295: Four by Four (coffee at Tim Hortons)

M1295: Four creams and four sugars


SS1296: Card shark

M1296: Someone who is really good at playing cards


SS1297: Pool shark

M1297: Someone who is really good at playing

billiards


SS1298: Cut me some slack

M1298: Be nice to me


SS1299: Get off my case

M1299: Be nice to me

SS1300: Don't fool around

M1300: Don't waste time

SS1301: Don't fart around

M1301: Don't waste time

SS1302: Fuss pot

M1302: Picky person

SS1303: Does not even touch the surface

M1303: Much more to know

SS1304: Does not even scratch the surface

M1304: Much more to know

SS1305: Staying up

M1305: Staying awake

SS1306: Taking it easy

M1306: Relaxing


SS1307: Yet to be seen

M1307: Evidence to come


SS1308: Just scraping by

M1308: In financial need


SS1309: In the poor house

M1309: In financial need


SS1310: It takes all kinds

M1310: The world is full of different people


SS1311: Lame duck

M1311: One that does not do anything

SS1312: The end of the line

M1312: Cannot go any further


SS1313: Bullshit artist

M1313: Someone who lies a lot


SS1314: A person throwing their weight around

M1314: An aggressive person


SS1315: They have baggage

M1315: Bad past


SS1316: Rocking the cradle

M1316: Dating someone much younger than
       yourself

SS1317: City slicker

M1317: A person from a city or urban center


SS1318: Hick

M1318: A person from the country or rural area


SS1319: Your better half

M1319: Your partner or significant other


SS1320: Stool pigeon

M1320: A person who reveals secrets


SS1321: A whipping boy

M1321: Somebody being used


SS1322: South paw

M1322: A person who is left-handed

SS1323: The real McCoy

M1323: The real or authentic thing


SS1324: Screwball

M1324: An idiot


SS1325: Bullshit

M1325: I do not believe you


SS1326: Not up to scratch

M1326: Not up to expectations


SS1327: You got nailed

M1327: You got caught


SS1328: Blarney

M1328: Exaggerating the truth

SS1329: True blue

M1329: Honest


SS1330: Justice is blind

M1330: Can't see the truth


SS1331: Mending fences

M1331: Resolving differences


SS1332: Turn a blind eye

M1332: Overlook an offence


SS1333: Heard it through the grapevine

M1333: Gossip


SS1334: Going Dutch

M1334: Splitting or paying the bill equally

SS1335: Turn coat

M1335: Traitor


SS1336: White elephant

M1336: Incomplete


SS1337: Kangaroo court

M1337: Predictable court


SS1338: Scuttle but

M1338: Gossiper


SS1339: Charlie Horse

M1339: Tightened muscles


SS1340: For the birds

M1340: It is no good

SS1341: Scapegoat

M1341: Somebody who takes the blame


SS1342: Well heeled

M1342: Lots of money


SS1343: You are a monkey's uncle

M1343: Astonished


SS1344: Till the cows come home

M1344: Waiting awhile


SS1345: Nest egg

M1345: A good amount of savings


SS1346: Every dog has its day

M1346: It may happen back to you

SS1347: Somebody who takes the hit

M1347: Somebody who takes the blame


SS1348: Knock on wood

M1348: Good luck


SS1349: Two bits

M1349: A quarter


SS1350: Hob knobbing

M1350: Hanging out with influential people


SS1351: Black mail

M1351: Holding someone at ransom by threating

to reveal their secrets if they do not pay

you money

SS1352: Eaves dropping

M1352: Listening to someone else's private conversation

SS1353: You are a laughing stock

M1353: Target of ridicule

SS1354: Talking gibberish

M1354: Talking nonsense

SS1355: A saw buck

M1355: Five dollars

SS1356: Hanging out

M1356: Spending time together

SS1357: A square meal

M1357: A fulfilling meal


SS1358: Chow time

M1358: Time to eat


SS1359: You got sacked

M1359: You got fired


SS1360: When my ship comes in

M1360: When I can afford it


SS1361: A stand up person

M1361: A legitimate and genuine person

SS1362: Stole his thunder

M1362: Took credit for another person's

recognition


SS1363: To put a kibosh on things

M1363: Abruptly put to a stop


SS1364: Slush fund

M1364: Money set aside to pay off people to keep

them quiet or for pleasure


SS1365: Petty cash

M1365: Money set aside


SS1366: S.O.S

M1366: Help

SS1367: Hitting the hay

M1367: Going to sleep


SS1368: Sixth sense

M1368: Intuition


SS1369: The coast is clear

M1369: No interference


SS1370: The third degree

M1370: Intensely examine or accuse


SS1371: Putting on the dog

M1371: Pretending you are somebody that you

are not

SS1372: Does not have a clue

M1372: Does not have an idea or know what is

going on


SS1373: Cheated the devil

M1373: Survived a disaster


SS1374: Pushing the envelope

M1374: Expanding the limits


SS1375: Won't pass the acid test

M1375: Won't be approved


SS1376: On target

M1376: On time or schedule

SS1377: Zonked out

M1377: Feel asleep after being really tired


SS1378: Crashed out at their place

M1378: Slept over at someone else's home


SS1379: Don't have a bird

M1379: Don't get upset


SS1380: Wise as an owl

M1380: Very wise


SS1381: I've got chump change

M1381: Mixed loose change; not much money


SS1382: Put your head in the sand

M1382: Ashamed and hide

SS1383: Proud as a peacock

M1383: Very proud


SS1384: Out in no man's land

M1384: Lost with no support


SS1385: Hail Mary

M1385: Last minute effort for a quick win


SS1386: Give them an inch and they take a mile

M1386: Taken advantage of


SS1387: Mouth off

M1387: To speak against


SS1388: Back talk

M1388: Reply rudely

SS1389: Damned if you do; damned if you don't

M1389: Can't win either way


SS1390: Heading in the wrong direction in life

M1390: Heading for trouble


SS1391: Cut my losses short

M1391: Stop before I lose more


SS1392: Grease monkey

M1392: An automobile mechanic


SS1393: Band aid solution

M1393: Temporary solution


SS1394: There going under

M1394: Going out of business

SS1395: Do the leg work

M1395: Do all the work


SS1396: Long and hard

M1396: A lot of difficult time to pass


SS1397: Short and sweet

M1397: Not a lot of time and good


SS1398: The tide is turning

M1398: Bad to good


SS1399: Putting out fires

M1399: Solving problems


SS1400: Can't string two thoughts together

M1400: Can't think